COMMAND
BLOCKS

HACKS FOR
MINECRAFTERS

COMMAND BLOCKS

HACKS FOR MINECRAFTERS

THE UNOFFICIAL GUIDE TO TIPS AND TRICKS THAT OTHER GUIDES WON'T TEACH YOU

MEGAN MILLER
with ANTHONY HEDDINGS

Sky Pony Press
New York

Copyright © 2015 by Hollan Publishing, Inc.

First box set edition 2016.

Minecraft® is a registered trademark of Notch Development AB

The Minecraft game is copyright © Mojang AB

Sky Pony Press books may be purchased in bulk at special discounts for sales promotion, corporate gifts, fund-raising, or educational purposes. Special editions can also be created to specifications. For details, contact the Special Sales Department, Sky Pony Press, 307 West 36th Street, 11th Floor, New York, NY 10018 or info@skyhorsepublishing.com.

Sky Pony® is a registered trademark of Skyhorse Publishing, Inc.®, a Delaware corporation.

Minecraft® is a registered trademark of Notch Development AB.
The Minecraft game is copyright © Mojang AB.

Visit our website at www.skyponypress.com.

10 9 8 7 6 5 4 3 2 1

Library of Congress Cataloging-in-Publication Data is available on file.

Cover photo credit: Megan Miller

TABLE OF CONTENTS

INTRODUCTION

Welcome to the slightly crazy world of commands and command blocks. With commands, you can do all kinds of things that aren't possible in a regular Survival world. You can create a super-powerful zombie or a villager that will trade diamonds for dirt, build towers of emerald blocks, and instantly teleport to any location.

This book will show you how commands work, and it will look at the most popular commands for creating fun creatures and effects, whether playing by yourself or creating a map for others to play. You'll also see how you can use command blocks to create commands that anyone in your multiplayer world can use.

Because commands can very easily be typed incorrectly, I've created a text document (.txt) that contains the commands referenced in this book. You can download this text document from meganfmiller.com/commands. You can copy and paste the commands from the document into your own command blocks. However, you will need to check each command to see if there are any values you need to change so that the command works in your game and on your server. These are values like XYZ locations (where the command should occur) and player names. For creating your own custom commands, it can often be easiest to use an online command generator, and the addresses to several of these generators are included in this book.

There's no undo button in Minecraft.

Commands are very powerful, and some can change your world significantly. Remember that there's no undo button in Minecraft. As you are starting to use and understand commands and how they work, use a test world that you won't mind losing if disaster strikes. I've included instructions for creating a test world in the first chapter.

Lastly, some commands are a little different in varying versions of Minecraft. The commands in this book are created for Minecraft 1.9.

CHAPTER 1

WHAT IS A COMMAND?

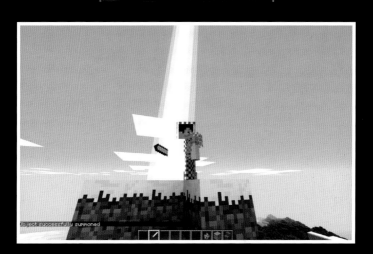

A command, in Minecraft and many other computer programs, is a string of very specific words that the software is programmed to react to. Some commands in Minecraft give you items you wouldn't normally get playing a game in Survival mode, so these are sometimes called cheats.

For example, you can use the /xp command to give a player any amount of experience points (XP). That's pretty cheaty, but in a special mini-game, giving XP can be a great reward to players who have accomplished some specific feat.

There are commands for doing all different types of things in Minecraft. Some commands are used only by an operator, or op, for managing, allowing, and banning players on the server. These commands aren't available to use in command blocks. Other commands can only be used on players (like giving them XP) or on blocks (like putting a block at a specific location). There are also commands that affect the whole world, like changing it to nighttime or daytime. We'll look at these different types of commands (except for the server management commands) and how to use them in the following chapters.

NOTE: To use commands in a single-player world, you must either be playing in Creative mode or have created your world with cheats on. If you are playing on multiplayer, you must be a server administrator or operator (op).

You use commands in Minecraft in the chat window. For example, to give yourself 30 XP levels, you open the chat window by pressing T. Then type:

```
/xp 30L
```

You type in the chat window, at your screen's bottom left, to give a command.

This simple command gives whoever types it 30 full levels of XP, enough for the best enchantments!

Other commands are more complicated, and you must include ID numbers or names and codes that reference specific traits or other variables. For example, to create a tame black horse with white spots, a couple blocks away from you and wearing a saddle and diamond armor, you would type:

```
/summon EntityHorse ~ ~1 ~ {Type:0,Tame:1,
Variant:516,ArmorItem:{id:diamond_horse_
armor},SaddleItem:{id:saddle}}
```

To summon a tame horse with a specific color, markings, and armor takes a much longer command than granting someone XP.

The next chapter, Command Rules (or Syntax), will look at all the various parts of a command and how you put a command together.

Setting Up a New World

If you are playing and practicing with commands and command blocks, it can be helpful to set up a Superflat Creative world. The Superflat world is . . . super flat! There are no mountains, ravines, or rivers that can make it difficult to set up special areas or to concentrate on building.

To set up a new single-player Superflat Creative world to use for playing with command blocks:

1. Start Minecraft, or quit your current game, so that you are at the opening Minecraft screen. Choose Singleplayer to open up the Select World screen.

2. On the Select World screen, click Create New World.

3. In the Create New World screen, type in the name of your world (this could be something descriptive, like Command Block World). Click the Game Mode button until it says Game Mode Creative. Click More World Options.

4. In the World Options screen, click the World Type button until it reads "Superflat" and then click the Customize button that appears.

5. In the Superflat customization screen, click Presets to open the Select a Preset screen.

6. In the Select a Preset screen that opens, type the following into the top text box. (You may be able to correct the type that is already there, or just delete any existing text.)

```
3;minecraft:bedrock,52xminecraft:dirt,
minecraft:grass;1;
```

7. Click Use Preset. In the Customization screen that displays again, you should see that the layers for your world are 1 grass at the top, 52 dirt in the middle, and 1 bedrock at the bottom.

8. Click Done to exit the Customization screen.
9. Click Done to exit the World Options screen.
10. Click Create New World to create your command block world.

CHAPTER 2

COMMAND RULES (OR SYNTAX)

For a command to work, you have to use only the proper words for that command, and these words must be in a specific order. These rules for how you type a command are called syntax. Each Minecraft command has a syntax that you must follow. (If you don't, the command may not work or may do something unexpected.)

Basically, you type the name of the command, followed by parameters. Parameters are words or numerical values that specify more about who, what, and where the command acts on. You may also hear these words referred to as *specifiers*.

The syntax for a command describes what words and parameters belong in the command and in what order they should be typed, along with the spaces and punctuation needed between words.

For example, the syntax for the /summon command is:

```
/summon <EntityName> [x][y][z] [dataTag]
```

This means that the summon command must start with a slash and the word summon. After one space (the spaces are important!) it must be followed by an entity name. You can also add coordinates in the XYZ format to indicate the location at which to create the entity. Finally, you can add additional data tags for more attributes of the entity.

You don't have to type in values for every parameter. The syntax is written in a way that makes it clear what you do have to type and what is optional:

> **Regular text** = You must type anything in regular (not italic or slanting) text.
>
> *Italic text* = Parameters you replace with your own values
>
> **<Angle brackets>** = Parameters you must replace. Don't include the angle brackets.
>
> **[Square brackets]** = Parameters you don't have to replace. Don't include the square brackets.
>
> **optionA | optionB** = You must choose one out of the options shown.

IMPORTANT: Although you can omit parameters that are in square brackets, you must type in values for all parameters that are located before any used parameter. This is the only way the software knows what values belong to which parameter. In other words, once you omit a parameter, you can't include any parameters after this.

An Example Command
- -

Look at this simple way to use the /summon command.

`/summon Villager`

The command begins with a slash (/). Any commands you type in a chat window have to start with a slash. If you're using a command block, you can leave the slash out, either way.

Notice there are only two words: the command name and one parameter—the required parameter, EntityName. Both of these are typed in regular text in the syntax, so you know they are necessary. But you don't type the parameter name EntityName. In the syntax, it was typed in italics, so you just replace the parameter with the actual value you want. (When you replace a parameter with the value you want, the value is often called the argument.) Here, you must type the official entity name that Minecraft assigned to the entity you want. This command is for a villager, so I used the villager's entity name, which is "Villager" with a capital V.

This simple command doesn't list any specific traits or career the villager should have, or where the villager should appear. So this command creates a random villager at the default location, which is wherever you (or a command block) are located in the world.

A More Complicated Example Command

A more complex version of the /summon command is:

```
/summon Villager 340 69 -220 {CustomName:
Fred,Profession:Profession:3,Career:3}
```

This command adds more parameters after the entity name Villager:

- **340 69 -220** These three numbers specify the XYZ coordinates to spawn the villager at. (And unless you're near that location, you won't see this villager being created!) Notice how these are typed with spaces in between. We'll go over how to use coordinates in commands and command blocks.

- **CustomName:Fred** This is a data tag that changes the name of the villager to Fred. The set of data tags starts with a curly bracket. The next chapter looks at how you use and format these data tags properly.

- **Profession:Profession:3,Career:3** This data tag says the villager's career should be Profession 3 (Blacksmith) and Career 3 (Tool Smith).

You can add a custom name to almost everything in Minecaft. This villager's custom name was added with the entity dataTag "CustomName".

Specifying Blocks, Entities, and Items

So if you have the syntax of a command, how do you know what values you can use for the parameters? What can you use for EntityName, besides Villager? We'll go over what your options are with each command we look at.

Pretty much each type of "thing" in Minecraft, from creepers to diamond ore to chests, falls into one of three main categories: blocks, items, and entities. Each object has a special ID name and/or ID number that you use in commands to specify that object. For each command, the explanations for the command syntax will tell you whether to use an ID name or an ID number. Most command syntaxes will call for an ID name, because Minecraft has been changing the code for commands to use the ID names rather than the numbers.

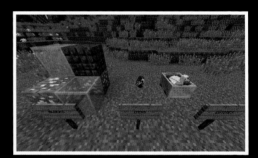

Almost all objects in Minecraft are categorized into three main categories: blocks (left), items (middle), and entities (right).

The appendices at the back of this book list many of these objects and their ID names and ID numbers. This means that when you look at a command syntax that asks for an <Item>, you can look in the Item ID appendix to find the ID for the item you want. When a command syntax asks you to use a Block ID, you can look in the Block ID appendix.

It's very important to type a command with no spelling, spacing, punctuation, capitalization, or other typing errors (typos).

If you don't, the command will either fail or give you unexpected results. For example, you could accidentally type in the wrong world coordinates to which to teleport a player. Wrong coordinates can lead to burning in a lava pool or suffocating inside an extreme hill!

When you enter a command into the Chat window, you will get a system notice saying whether it failed or succeeded. The exact message you get depends on the command you used, but a fail message will always be in red.

If you type a command incorrectly you will get a fail message. If you type it correctly, you will get a success message even if you use wrong information, like the wrong coordinates. So a success message doesn't always mean the command worked the way you wanted it to.

If your Minecraft chat window gets too busy with notices and announcements, you can clear it by pressing F3 and D.

When you are typing commands, try to think of each word not as a whole word but as a string of foreign characters. You have to look at every character, including spaces, to make sure it is the right one and is in the right order. One character missing is a fail, because programs like games aren't built to autocorrect spelling and punctuation.

Using Auto-Complete

The chat system's auto-complete can help you with typing some of your commands. You use the Tab key to have Minecraft show you what commands, or commands and specifiers, match what you've typed. (Auto-complete doesn't work if there is anything typed on the right side of the text cursor.)

- Type / and press Tab to cycle through available commands.

- Type / and the first few letters and then press Tab to see commands that match those letters.

- Type /, the command, and press Space. Now press Tab to see what parameters can follow the command.

If you type the slash and the first letter or letters of the command, and then press Tab, Chat will display the first possible command that has the same first letter(s). You can press Tab again to get more matches. After you type a command (and the space that comes after it), you can press Tab again to see what additional options there are, if any.

For example, to have Minecraft help you with the /gamemode command:

1. Type /g and press Tab. Continue pressing Tab until the chat window shows /gamemode.

2. Press the space bar to add a space.

3. Press Tab again to have Minecraft show the possible arguments for /gamemode. Stop when you see /gamemode creative.

4. Your command is complete, and now you can press Enter to execute it and switch to Creative mode.

You can press Tab when you are typing a command into the chat window to see suggestions in the notification area.

To have Minecraft help you with the name of a block or item, type "minecraft:" in the location of the command where you are inserting the block or item name. For example, type /give meganfairminecraft:m and press Tab to see all the items you can give that start with M.

For all the block and item ID names, you can add the word "minecraft:" (with a colon at the end and no spaces) in front of it. For example "minecraft:dirt" is the same as "dirt". Using "minecraft:" in the chat window allows the auto-complete function to help you with items.

Get Outside Help!

There are lots of command generators online that you can use to help you with your command. They have a form you fill out to select commands, parameters, and arguments. When you are finished, you usually click a button, and a text box will show you your finished command. Copy (Ctrl/Command+C) this text, go to Minecraft, and paste (Ctrl/Command+V) this copied command into the chat window or into a command block. With online generators, you do need to make sure that the generator works with your version of Minecraft.

Some online generators are:

http://www.minecraftupdates.com/commands

http://minecraft.tools

http://mcstacker.bimbimma.com

CHAPTER 3

CUSTOMIZING COMMANDS

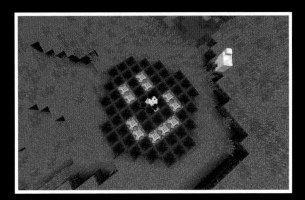

In Chapter 2, you saw how parameters are used with commands. Choosing values (or arguments) for some parameters is fairly simple, like choosing a Block Name. Others, like <X Y Z>, target selectors, and <dataTag>, are a bit more complex. There are a number of ways to use values for these.

XYZ Coordinates

The XYZ coordinates that you use in a command show the exact place in the world at which the command should take place or create something, along imaginary lines called axes. When you use XYZ coordinates, there's always an imaginary center at 0 0 0. In Minecraft, 0 0 0 is set to be around your original spawn point.

The Debug screen shows you the coordinates where you are standing, the block you are standing on, and the block you are looking at.

- **X:** Where you are on an east–west (X) line or axis. This number is negative when the location is west of the center.

- **Y:** Where you are on a vertical axis. This number is negative when the location is below the center.

- **Z:** Where you are on a north–south axis. This is negative when the location is north of the center.

The X-axis (red) shows where you are on an east–west imaginary line. The Y-axis (green) shows you where you are vertically. The Z-axis (blue) shows you where you are along a north–south line.

To find a coordinate, open up your debug screen by pressing F. Look for these entries in the bottom left section

- **XYZ:** This entry shows exactly where you are standing, with decimals.

- **Block:** This shows the XYZ coordinates for the block you are standing on.

- **Facing:** This shows which way you are looking.

- **Looking at:** This shows what block your cursor is pointing at. This entry only shows up when you are close enough to a block that it shows a thin line around it.

So when you need to enter a real XYZ coordinate for a command, you can go to the location you want it to appear. If you want it to appear above the block you are standing on or looking at, you'll have to add 1 for each block you are raising the location.

Relative Coordinates

You can also use relative locations. These say where the XYZ location should be in relation to where the command was given. This is either where you are when you enter the command in chat or where the command block is.

You specify an XYZ location with a tilde (~). The key for this squiggly line is usually at the top left of your keyboard. You use three tildes by themselves, in place of the XYZ coordinates, to set the location at the command-giver's location. You can also type a number, positive or negative, after any tilde to specify the distance in blocks, along that axis, away from the command-giver's location.

~ ~ ~: This makes command execute at the location of the command-giver.

~1 ~ ~-2: In this example, the X is ~1. This says the command must execute 1 block east (because it is a positive number) of the command-giver. The Y is the tilde by itself. So this says to execute the command at the same vertical (Y) position as the command-giver. Finally, the ~-2 for the Z position says that the command should execute 2 blocks north (because it is a negative number) of the command-giver's location.

Use the Debug screen (F3) to find coordinates for the block you are standing on and a block you are looking at.

Target Selectors

Some commands allow you to use target selectors. Target selectors let you select one or more players or entities without knowing their exact locations or names. You use a special target variable instead of a name or ID.

@p   This selects the nearest person to the command-giver.

@r   This selects a random player in the world.

@a   This selects all players in the world.

@e   This selects all entities in the world (including players).

You can also be more specific by using arguments with a target selector. Target selector arguments include:

x y z	Selects targets only at these XYZ coordinates (You can't use relative coordinates.)
r, rm	Selects targets only within the radius r from the XYZ coordinates. Rm selects targets only outside the radius.
c	Selects targets up to a certain amount (count)
m	Selects targets by gamemode. Doing [m=!*gamemode*] will select targets not on a certain game mode. A value of -1 will select all game modes.
l, lm	Selects targets with no more than a certain XP level. Lm selects targets with no less than a certain XP level.
name	Selects targets that match an entity name (either a player name or an entity that has been give a custom name)
type	Selects targets that match an entity type
dx dy dz	Selects targets within a large box. The box is dx wide, dz long, and dy high and has a corner at the location the command was executed
score_ *name*	Selects targets with a scoreboard value in the objective "name" of no more than a certain amount
score_ name_min	Selects targets with a scoreboard value in the objective "name" of no less than a certain amount
team	Selects targets only on a certain team. Doing [team= !*teamname*] will select targets not on a certain team.
tag	Selects targets with a certain scoreboard tag. Doing [tag=!*tag*] will select targets without a certain tag.

When you use arguments for a target selector, you have to use argument:value pairs. These argument:value pair or pairs have to be enclosed in square brackets and typed without spaces. If there's more than one pair, you use a comma with no space to separate the pairs. Here are some examples of using a target selector, with the commands /xp and /tp (teleport):

/xp 2L @p Gives 2 XP levels to the nearest player to the command-giver

/xp 2L @p[x=-697,y=65,z=211] Gives 2 XP levels to the nearest player to the X Y Z location of -697 65 211.

/tp @a @r Teleports everyone to one random player's location

/tp @e [type=Creeper,c=4] @r Teleports up to 4 entities that match the type creeper to a random player. Very mean!

Working with Data Tags

Some advanced or complicated commands can have long strings of data tag parameters in them. These data tags help define the traits or properties of items, blocks, and entities. Data tags are grouped and enclosed in either square or curly brackets:

[List Tags]: Tags that are lists, or can have several values separated by commas, use square brackets. The square brackets let the computer software know that what follows is a list, and commas separate each different value.

{Compound Tags}: Tags that are defined as "compound tags" use curly brackets. A compound tag has an identifying parameter name, such as "id", followed by a colon ":", followed by a space and then the value "1". The curly brackets let the computer software know to expect this type of information and when it ends.

Data Tags and Data Values

Data tags are different from data values. Data tags are attribute: value pairs that describe various characteristics of an item or entity. Data values are additional ID numbers that specify a type of block or item. For example, the ID name for granite is stone, so its data value (DV)—which is 1—defines it as a granite block.

Here's an example of a very long command that gives the nearest player a chest with a couple of items in it:

```
/give @p chest 1 0 {BlockEntityTag: {Items:
[{id:stone,Slot: 0,Count: 23},{id:wool,Damage:
1,Slot: 1,Count: 12},{id:torch,Slot: 2,Count:
1},{id:diamond_sword,  Slot: 3,  Count: 1}]}}
```

Each item (starting with "id") is surrounded by curly brackets, and the list of items (after "Items") is enclosed by square brackets. Everything that the data tag "BlockEntityTag" refers to is also enclosed with curly brackets. Finally, all the dataTag parameters (everything after the "data" argument of 0) are enclosed in another pair of curly brackets.

The data values that you can use for different entities and items depend on that object. The Minecraft Wiki has a long list of what data tags (also called NBT tags) work with what item or entity, at http://minecraft.gamepedia.com/Chunk_format, under the heading NBT Structure.

Balancing Brackets

It is very important to make sure each opening bracket has a closing bracket to match it, at the right place. It is also incredibly easy to forget a bracket. Simple code editing software, like Atom for Mac or Notepad++ for Windows, can help highlight brackets that match or are missing. You can also use a regular text editor (TextEdit in Mac or Notepad in Windows) to write out long commands in a way that shows where the brackets are, so you can make sure they are balanced.

```
/give @p chest 1 0 {
    BlockEntityTag: {
        Items: [
            {
                id:stone,
                Slot: 0,
                Count: 23
            },
            {
                id:wool,
                Damage: 1,
                Slot: 1,
                Count: 12
            },
            {
                id:torch,
                Slot: 2,
                Count: 1
            },
            {
                id: diamond_sword,
                Slot: 3,
                Count: 1
            }
        ]
    }
}
```

In this notation, you put the brackets on separate lines, and indent pairs of brackets, so you can clearly see each pair of brackets and what they contain.

CHAPTER 4

USING COMMAND BLOCKS

Command blocks are blocks that you place in the Minecraft world. Each command block can have one command assigned to it. To execute the command, you activate the block by sending it a redstone signal. The simplest way to do this is to place a button on the actual command block.

Differences between Command Blocks and Chat Commands

- Command blocks can take very long commands, while Chat entries are limited to 100 characters.

- Players without op status can execute commands in command blocks. (Only ops can place commands in command boxes, though.)

- Command blocks are much more powerful than Chat commands since you can control them with redstone.

- Two or more commands can be linked together by linking command blocks with redstone or using chain command blocks.

- Using relative coordinates in a command block means the location will be relative to the command block, not where you are.

Getting Command Blocks

Command blocks are very powerful, so they aren't available by crafting or in the Creative inventory. You have to use a command in the Chat window to get them. To give yourself a stack of 64 command blocks, type the following into the chat window:

```
/give  @p  minecraft:command_block 64
```

Adding Commands to Command Blocks

You must be in Creative mode to add commands to command blocks. To assign a command to a command block:

1. Place the block on the ground where you want it to be. Remember that its location will determine where any relative coordinates point to.

2. Right-click the command to open the command block interface.

3. Type (or paste) the command into the Console Command text box. (The box below is where the command block shows success or error messages for the last executed command. You can turn this off by clicking the button 0 to make it X.)

4. Click Done to assign the command and close the interface.

You type a command into the Console Command text box at the top of the command block interface.

Types of Command Blocks

There are three different kinds of command blocks. The default command block is orange and is called an Impulse command block. Impulse command blocks execute their commands only when they receive redstone signal.

If you place down an Impulse command block, you can change its type by right-clicking it to open the interface and clicking on the button that says "Impulse".

The other two types of command blocks are Repeat and Chain.
Repeat command blocks will execute their command every tick
(20 times a second!). This is useful if you want a command to
always be running.

Be careful with what commands you put into Repeat command
blocks! If you put a /give command, your inventory would
quickly fill up!

Here's a fun command to try with Repeat command blocks.
Grab a few snowballs and a few boats, and put this command
into a repeat command block:

```
/execute @e[type=Snowball] ~ ~-4 ~ /fill ~-2
~ ~-2 ~2 ~ ~2 minecraft:water 0 replace air
```

Make sure to click the "Needs Redstone" button to change it to
"Always Active". This command will make a pool of water below
every snowball you throw! It can get out of hand pretty quick,
but it's fun to ride around on the towers of water with a boat.

You might see your chat fill up with messages from command blocks. To turn this off, run:

```
/gamerulecommandBlockOutput false
```

WARNING: Using a Repeat command block to loop a command over and over again can use up too much memory and can crash your game or machine. When you are experimenting, use a test world that you don't mind losing if something goes wrong, or make a backup of your world.

The other type of command block is Chain. Chain command blocks are placed in a line, and when the first one in the line is activated, the next one activates, going down the line in order. This is useful for making chains or commands that need to be in order.

Activating and Linking Command Blocks

To activate an Impulse command block, you have to send it a redstone signal. While redstone is too big a topic to cover in this book, there are simple solutions for activating command blocks. You basically just need to attach a power source to the block and turn it on. For example:

1. Place a button or lever on the block. You will need to hold shift while right-clicking to do this. The lever has two positions, on and off, so you click it once to turn the signal on. Then, to repeat the command, you have to turn it off, and then back on again. The button automatically turns itself off, so each time you press it the block will execute the command. Make sure the command block is on Impulse, not Repeat!

2. Place a button or lever on another non-transparent block, and connect that block to the command block with redstone dust. The line of redstone dust must point directly at the command block.

Combining Command Blocks

You can connect command blocks in a line by setting the command blocks to Conditional. A Conditional command block will only run its command if the block behind it ran its command with no errors. They're a lot like Chain command blocks, except Chain command blocks don't check if a command failed or not, and you can use Repeat command blocks in the conditional chain as well.

You can also combine command blocks to the outside world with a redstone signal that links to each one, with redstone dust and/or redstone repeaters. A redstone repeater needs to face into the command block to send it a signal.

You can activate several command blocks at the same time by connecting them all to a single button, lever, or other power source.

TIP: It can be easy to forget what a command block does. Add a sign next to your command blocks that reminds you what each of them does.

CHAPTER 5

BASIC COMMANDS

Some commands are very simple, general commands. Some of these can be used by anyone, not just an op. Basic commands include:

/difficulty
/gamemode
/help
/list
/me
/say
/tell

This command sets the difficulty level of the current game, which can be Peaceful, Easy, Normal, or Hard.

For example, you might use one command block to change your Normal Survival world to Peaceful, in order to kill all hostile mobs. When you are done playing in Peaceful, use a second command block to change the world back to Normal to set your game back to Survival mode. You can also connect these two command blocks with redstone, so that you first change to Peaceful to kill hostiles and then go immediately back to your Normal Survival mode.

Syntax

```
/difficulty <difficulty level>
```

- Replace <difficulty level> with one of the following:
    - peaceful (or p or 0)
    - easy (or e or 1)
    - normal (or n or 2)
    - hard (or h or 3)

Examples

```
/difficulty peaceful
/difficulty 1
/difficulty h
```

The /gamemode Command

This command changes a player's current gamemode to Survival, Creative, Adventure, or Spectator. (Hardcore isn't a true game mode—it combines Hard difficulty level with having only one life in a world.) This can be handy in a game map, where you want to change a player from Adventure mode to Spectator mode if they die (and are out of the game).

Syntax

```
/gamemode <mode> [player]
```

- Replace <mode> with one of the following:
    - o survival (or s or 0)
    - o creative (or c or 1)
    - o adventure (or a or 2)
    - o spectator (or sp or 3)

- May replace [player] with the username of a single player or a target selector. If you don't specify a player, you will change your own game mode. If you are using this in a command block, you must specify a player.

Examples

```
/gamemode s meganfair
/gamemode 0 notch
/gamemode c
/gamemode sp @p
```

The /help Command

Any player can use the /help command to get information about commands. You can type /help for a list of all commands (for pages beyond 1, also type the page number). You can also get help for a specific command by typing the command name after help.

Syntax

```
/help [page|commandname]
```

- Replace [page/commandname] with either a number from 1 to 7 for that page of help text or with the name of the command.

Examples

```
/help
/help 3
/help give
```

The /list Command

Any player can use the /list command, which simply lists all the players that are currently playing. You can also press the Tab key for the same information.

Syntax

```
/list
```

The /me Command

Any player can use this command to send a message to other players. This "me" message always begins with your user name.

Syntax

```
/me <any text>
```

- Replace <any text> with the text of your choice. You can include target selectors, like @p.

Example

```
/me makes sadface
```

This displays as: *meganfair makes sadface.

Notice that the message display starts with an asterisk (*) before your username. This lets other players know that the message is coming from another player.

If you are an op, you can also use target selectors in the <any text> you include. This will result in one or more targets' usernames being displayed. Also, if you use this in a command block, the message displayed will replace "/me" with "@". @ is the default name of the command block, but you can rename a command block with an anvil. Then the /me command will use the command block's given name. So, if you name a command block "The Flying Spaghetti Monster" and have it execute this command, it will show in Chat as:

*The Flying Spaghetti Monster makes sadface.

The /say Command

The /say command sends a message in the chat screen to all players. This is almost identical to a chat message, but you can use target selectors like @p to include usernames in the message. If a command block is programmed with the /say command, it will use "@" as its display name. You can rename the command block with an anvil to change the command block's name. A second difference from a chat message is that the sayer's name is enclosed in square brackets, rather than the angled brackets used for names in Chat. You can use this with command blocks to give general announcements or make it seem like a message is coming from someone else—whatever you name the command block.

Syntax

`/say <any text>`

- Replace <any text> with your message.

Examples

`/say The server will shut down for maintenance at 5pm EST`

If I type this, the Chat will show:

[meganfair]The server will shut down for maintenance at 5pm EST

If a command block named "IMPORTANT" executes this, the Chat will show:

[IMPORTANT]The server will shut down for maintenance at 5pm EST

The /tell Command

Anyone can use the /tell command to send a private message to one or more players on the server. If an operator uses this command, he or she can use a target selector in place of usernames.

Syntax

```
/tell <player> <any text>
```

- Replace <player> with the username of the player you are sending the message to.
- Replace <any text> with your private message.

Example

```
/tell BigRabbit Do you want to play Death
Games?
```

If I send this message to player BigRabbit on my server, BigRabbit (and only BigRabbit) will see the following message:

meganfair whispers to you: Do you want to play Death Games?

CHAPTER 6

WORLD COMMANDS

World commands change something that affects the entire world or game. For example, the /weather command changes what the weather is, and the /time command changes what time it is in the game.

World commands include:

/defaultgamemode
/gamerule
/seed
/setworldspawn
/time
/toggledownfall
/weather
/worldborder

The /defaultgamemode Command

This command changes the game mode that new players on the server will be in: Survival, Creative, Adventure, or Spectator. You'd use this command on a multiplayer server, perhaps with an adventure map. You could use this command to make sure that every player that starts playing in the world is in Adventure mode, so that they can't break down buildings, for example.

In Spectator mode, you are invisible to other players. But if you press F5, you can see other players who are also in Spectator mode. You appear to each other as a transparent head floating around.

Syntax

```
/defaultgamemode <mode>
```

- Replace <mode> with one of the following arguments:
  - survival (or s or 0)
  - creative (or c or 1)
  - adventure (or a or 2)
  - spectator (or sp or 3)

Examples

```
/defaultgamemode adventure
/defaultgamemode 3
/defaultgamemode c
```

The /gamerule command lets you set basic game options for your world or find out the current game options. You can also create a new game rule that you can use to store a value that you can retrieve and use later. This would be useful if you are combining command blocks to make a command block program.

Syntax

`/gamerule <rulename>[value]`

- Replace <rulename> with one of the game rules listed below.

- May replace [value] with a valid value for the game rule you are setting. This will generally be either true, false, or a number. If you don't type a value for the rule here, then the response will tell you what the game rule is currently set to.

Gamerules*		
GameRule	**Description**	**Values**
commandBlockOutput	If true, command blocks notify administrators when they execute a command. The default value is true.	true or false
doDaylightCycle	This stops and starts the sun and moon moving. The default value is true. You might use this on a map where you want it to be daylight the entire day, so that fewer mobs spawn naturally.	true or false

GameRule	Description	Values
doMobLoot	This allows mobs to drop items when they are killed, like zombies dropping rotten flesh. The default value is true. Turning this off means you also won't get meat from passive mobs, so you'll have to be a vegetarian, too.	true or false
doMobSpawning	This decides whether mobs (including passive and neutral mobs) should naturally spawn. The default value is true. Mobs can still spawn from spawners if this is set to false.	true or false
keepInventory	If you change this to true, whenever someone dies, all their inventory will remain with them. The default value is false. You might turn this on in a special Survival mini-game, where players die constantly. This allows them to get back into the fight quickly with their sword or bow and arrow.	true or false

GameRule	Description	Values
mobGriefing	This allows mobs to destroy or change blocks, such as creepers blowing up the landscape or sheep "eating" grass blocks and turning them into dirt. It also allows mobs like villagers, Endermen, and zombies to pick up items. The default value is true.	true or false
naturalRegeneration	This lets players naturally get back health points, as long as their hunger bar is high enough. The default value is true.	true or false
showDeathMessages	This turns on and off messages displaying in Chat when a player dies. The default value is true.	true or false

*This list is a shortened version of the full list on the Minecraft Wiki, which you can find at http://minecraft.gamepedia.com/Commands#gamemode

Use the mobGriefing option to turn off damage from creepers and other block-changing mobs.

Examples

```
/gamerule mobGriefing false
/gamerule NewGameRule 30
```

The second example shows how you can create and save a new game rule.

The /seed Command

The /seed command displays the number for the world seed. If you used regular words for your seed, such as "awesome new world", the seed is still displayed as a number. This is because when you type in letters for a seed, the letters are converted into numbers. The seed is what helps the Minecraft software create entirely different worlds with new terrain. If you know the seed for your world, you can share the number with someone else. He or she can play the same world using your seed (you do have to be using the same version of Minecraft). Knowing the seed number can also help you find things like slime chunks. There are several online slime chunk finders that will take your seed number and let you know what areas slimes will spawn in (besides swamps at night). One slime finder is at chunkbase.com. (A chunk is a 16x16x256 block section of the world, used in the game programming.)

The slime chunks in your world are based on your world seed number. Slime chunks are 16x16 areas where slime will spawn at any light level, and below y=40.

`/seed`

There are no parameters or arguments for this command, just type /seed.

The /setworldspawn Command

The /setworldspawn command allows you to change the spawn location for your world. The spawn location is where new players appear and where you respawn when you die if you haven't slept in a bed somewhere. This can be helpful if the original world spawn is in an inhospitable area. If you've made a mini-game or adventure map, you may want players to start in a special location.

The /setworldspawn command lets you set the spawn for your world somewhere more convenient for you.

Syntax

`/setworldspawn [x y z]`

- May replace [x y z] with the coordinates you want. If you leave the command as /setworldspawn, then the location of the command block (or your location) will be set as spawn.

The /time Command

The /time command lets you change the time in your world to a specific time or to day or night. You can also use it to jump forward in time by a specific amount or find out how many ticks have gone by since midnight or the start of the world.

Time in Minecraft software is measured in ticks. There are 20 ticks in a second, so each tick lasts .05 of a second. Because a Minecraft full day/night cycle lasts 20 minutes in real time, this means there are a total of 24,000 ticks in a Minecraft day. From this, you can also determine that an in-game Minecraft hour lasts about 50 seconds in real time.

Syntax

`/time set <add|query|set> <value>`

- Replace <add|query|set> with one of the three options: add, query, or set.

- For "add", replace <value> with the number of ticks you want to add to the time, from 1 to 2147483647. To add a Minecraft hour, add 1000 ticks, and to add a day, add 24000.
- For "query", replace <value> with either "gametime" or "daytime". Gametime will return the total number of ticks since your world started, and daytime will return the number of ticks since midnight.
- For "set", replace <value> with either a number of ticks (from 0 to 2147483647), or day, or night. Setting the time to 1000 sets the time to day, and setting it to 13000 makes it nighttime.

Examples

```
/time set day
/time set 13000
/time add 24000
/time query gametime
```

The /toggledownfall Command

The /toggledownfall command is a simple command that lets you immediately start or stop downfall (rain or snow). If it is currently raining or snowing, the weather turns clear. If it is currently clear, it will start raining or snowing.

Syntax

`/toggledownfall`

There are no parameters for this command; you simply type /toggledownfall.

The /weather Command

You can use the /weather command to change the weather to clear, rain, or thunder. (If you are in a snowy biome, you'll get snow instead of rain. If you are in a desert biome, you won't see the rain, except at the borders to another biome.) The game will decide how long the weather will last. You can also set how long the weather should last before the game returns to its normal weather programming.

If you use the /weather rain command in the desert, you won't see any rain. But if you move just one block into another biome, it will be raining there.

Syntax

```
/weather <clear|rain|thunder> [number of
seconds]
```

- Replace <clear|rain|thunder> with one of the three options: clear, rain, or thunder.
- May replace [number of seconds] with a number from 1 to 1000000 to set how many seconds (in real time) the weather lasts.

Examples

```
/weather clear 1000000
/weather thunder
```

The /worldborder Commands

There are eight /worldborder commands. A world border is a boundary to the edge of a Minecraft world. World borders are used by mapmakers for special maps or for mini-games, like an Ultra Hardcore game. Sometimes regular multiplayer servers will use a world border at the start of a new map so that players build close together for a while and get to know each other. The world border is a square boundary, with its default center at 0,0, that limits players to play within it. This command refers to the length of the radius of the border (though the world border is a square). This is the distance from the center of the world border to one of the four side edges. World borders can also be set to grow or reduce in size. A static world border is aqua. An expanding border is green, and a contracting one is red.

If you accidentally create a world border, you can remove it by setting the worldborder to 30000000 (30 million).

/worldborder add

The /worldborder add command lets you increase the size of the current world border. You can also set how many seconds it will take to expand from the current border to the new border.

Syntax

```
/worldborder add <blocks>[seconds]
```

- Replace <blocks> with the number of blocks you are adding.
- Replace [seconds] with the number of seconds (in real time) the expansion should take.

Example

```
/worldborder add 100 3600
```

/worldborder center

The /worldborder center command lets you specify the center of the world border square. The default center is 0,0.

Syntax

```
/worldborder center <x><y>
```

- Replace <x> and <y> with the X and Y coordinates of the new center. Because world borders cover the whole height of the map, you do not need to set the Z coordinate.

Example

```
/worldborder center 100 -100
```

/worldborder damage amount

By default, a world border gives .2 points of damage to a player for each block the player goes beyond the border's buffer zone. This command allows you to specify how many damage points are given per block.

Syntax

```
/worldborder damage amount <damage points>
```

- Replace <damage points> with the number of damage points a player will be dealt for each block he or she goes beyond the buffer.

Example

```
/worldborder damage amount 1
```

/worldborder damage buffer

The default buffer zone for a world border is five blocks, and players aren't damaged until they get beyond this. This command lets you change how many blocks deep, or beyond the border, the buffer zone is.

Syntax

```
/worldborder damage buffer <blocks>
```

- Replace <blocks> with the new size, in blocks, of the buffer.

Example

```
/worldborder damage buffer 3
```

/worldborder get

The /worldborder get command displays the size of the world border.

Syntax

```
/worldborder get
```

There are no additional parameters for this command, you just type /worldborder get.

/worldborder set

The worldborder set command lets you create a world border with a specific size. You can also set how many seconds it takes for the border to grow or retreat to the new size.

Syntax

```
/worldborder set <sizeInBlocks>[seconds]
```

- Replace <sizeInBlocks> with the radius size you want. An entire side's length of the world border will be double this, so if you set a radius of 500, the new world border will make a play zone of 1000x1000.

- May replace [seconds] with the time, in real-time seconds, that it will take the current world border to change to the new size. (An hour is 3600 seconds.)

Example

```
/worldborder set 500 7200
```

Minecraft warns players about the world border by turning their screen red if they get close.

/worldborder warning distance

A world border will by default give a player a visual warning—the screen tints red—when they are within 5 blocks. This command allows you to set a different warning distance.

Syntax

```
/worldborder warning distance <sizeInBlocks>
```

- Replace <sizeInBlocks> with the distance from the border, in blocks, that a player will be warned.

Example
```
/worldborder warning distance 15
```

/worldborder warning time

If a world border is decreasing, and will reach a player within 15 seconds, that player will receive a warning. This command allows you to change the 15-second world border warning time.

Syntax

```
/worldborder warning time <seconds>
```

- Replace <seconds> with the amount of warning time a player should get for an approaching world border.

Examples

```
/worldborder warning time 120
```

CHAPTER 7

BLOCK COMMANDS

Block commands act on blocks. Blocks include all of the square cubes you can place in the world, from acacia wood planks to zombie heads. They also include crafted objects that you can place, like ladders and anvils. Block commands include:

/blockdata
/clone
/fill
/replaceitem
/setblock

The /blockdata Command

Some blocks have data tags to describe special attributes they have, beyond what type of block they are and their XYZ coordinates. Different blocks have different data tags. For example, a flowerpot has a data tag to describe if it's holding a flower or plant and what that plant is.

Syntax

```
/blockdata <x y z> <dataTag>
```

- Replace <x y z> with the coordinates of the block you are changing.
- Replace <dataTag> with the dataTag(s) you are changing. You have to use attribute-value pairs, for example: {Item:sapling}

Example

```
/blockdata ~ ~ ~1 {Item:sapling,Data:2}
```

The example command adds a spruce sapling to the flowerpot 1 block away.

The /clone command lets you copy blocks in a 3D area to another area. This is a terrific command for making copies of something that was hard to build, like a house or a complicated wall. You do have to be careful in figuring out the coordinates. You have to choose two opposite corner blocks of the area you are copying. Then, when you clone the area, you choose just one block for the destination location. The block you choose will be the lowest northwest corner of the new location. You won't be able to rotate your copy or make it face a different direction. You are also limited to a total number of 4,096 blocks to clone.

Syntax

```
/clone <x1 y1 z1> <x2 y2 z2> <x y z>
[maskMode] [cloneMode] [TileName]
```

- Replace <x1 y1 z1> with the XYZ coordinates at one corner of the area you are copying.

- Replace <x2 y2 z2> with the XYZ coordinates of the opposite area you are copying.

- Replace <x y z> with the XYZ coordinates of the location destination. The block you choose will be the lowest northwest corner of your copied area.

- May replace [maskMode] with one of the following:

  - **filtered:** You use this with the [Tilename] parameter to say which type of block should be copied. So you could copy only stone blocks, for example.

- ○ **masked:** This copies only blocks that are not air blocks.
- ○ **replace:** This copies all blocks. This is the default maskMode.

- May replace [cloneMode] with one of the following:

  - ○ **force:** This allows cloning to an overlapping area.
  - ○ **move:** This will fill the original area you are cloning with air blocks.
  - ○ **normal:** This is the default.

- If you are using the maskMode filtered, you must replace [TileName] with the ID name of the block type you want cloned.

The /clone command is a great way to make copies of buildings, like village houses, quickly.

Example

```
/clone -778 64 307 -774 68 310 -778 64 314
/clone -778 64 307 -774 68 310 ~2 ~ ~2
filtered normal sandstone
```

With the /fill command, you select a three-dimensional area and fill it with the block of your choice!

Syntax

```
/fill <x1 y1 z1> <x2 y2 z2> <TileName>
[dataValue] [oldBlockHandling] [dataTag]
[replaceTileName] [replaceDataValue]
```

- Replace <x1 y1 z1> and <x2 y2 z2> with the two opposite corners of your area.

- Replace <TileName> with the block ID name of the block you are using to fill the area.

- May replace [dataValue] with the data value for the block you are using.

- May replace [oldBlock Handling] with one of the following:

  - **destroy:** This makes the replaced blocks drop as if they were mined.
  - **hollow:** This replaces only the outside edges of the area with the new block and fills the interior with air blocks.
  - **keep:** This replaces only air blocks in the region with the new block.
  - **outline:** This is the same as hollow, except the interior blocks aren't changed.
  - **replace:** This is the default and replaces all blocks.

- May replace [dataTag] with a data tag for the new block. You cannot use this if you are using [replaceTileName] or [replaceDataValue].

- May replace [replaceTileName] with the type of block to replace in the region. This means, for example, that you can specify only to replace stone brick blocks with cobblestone blocks. This works only when you are using the oldBlockHandling value replace.

- May replace [replaceDataValue] with the data value of the tile to be replaced. This works only when you are using the oldBlockHandling value replace.

You can use the /fill command with the destroy option to clear a large area AND get the mining drops from it. Be careful though, Minecraft has no "Undo" button.

Examples

```
/fill -480 69 180 -500 89 200 diamond_ore
/fill ~2 ~ ~2 ~12 ~-5 ~12 air 0 destroy
```

This command modifies inventories of chests and players. You can use it to give items to players, refill dungeon chests, or equip mobs with weapons!

Syntax

```
/replaceitem block <x> <y> <z> <slot>
<item> [amount] [data] [dataTag]
```

This runs the command in block mode, which modifies chests, furnaces, and any block with an inventory.

You can also run it in entity mode, which modifies the inventories of players or mobs:

```
/replaceitem entity <selector> <slot>
<item> [amount] [data] [dataTag]
```

- In block mode, replace <x>, <y>, and <z> with the coordinates of the block you want to modify.

- In entity mode, replace <selector> with the player name or target selector of the entity you want to modify

- Replace <slot> with the number of the inventory slot you want to replace. Slot numbers for chests start at 0 in the top left corner and increase from left to right. Slot numbers for players are a little more complex.

- May replace [oldBlockHandling] with one of the following:

    ◦ For inventory slots, use slot.inventory. *slot_number*, where slot_number is the number from 0 to 26 of the slot you want to modify.

- ◦ For slots on the toolbar, use slot.hotbar. *slot_number*, where slot_number is the number from 0 to 8 of the slot you want to modify.

- ◦ For armor slots, use slot.armor.chest, slot. armor.head, slot.armor.feet, and slot.armor. legs. These don't need numbers.

- Replace <item> with the item name of the block you want to replace.

- May replace <amount> with the amount of blocks you want to replace.

- May replace [data] and [dataTag] with the damage value and data tag of the block you want to replace.

Examples

```
/replaceitem block ~2 ~ ~ 0 minecraft:
diamond_sword
```

Replace the first slot in a chest next to you with a new diamond sword.

```
/replaceitem entity @a slot.hotbar.8
minecraft:stone 64
```

Replace the last item in each players toolbar with a stack of stone. Useful for building!

This command changes a specific block in the world into a different type of block.

Syntax

`/setblock <x y z> <TileName> [dataValue] [oldBlockHandling] [dataTag]`

- Replace <x y z> with the XYZ coordinates of the block you are changing.

- Replace <TileName> with the ID name of the new block.

- May replace [dataValue] with any data value that you need to specify the new block.

- May replace [oldBlockHandling] with one of the following:

  ○ **destroy:** This makes the old block drop as if it were mined.
  ○ **keep:** This will only change the block if it is an air block.
  ○ **replace:** This is the default.

- May replace [dataTag] with the data tag for the new block.

Example

`/setblock -489 89 187 planks 3`

(This will change the existing block at this location to a jungle block.)

CHAPTER 8

ENTITY COMMANDS

Entity commands are commands you can use on entities. Entities are moving objects in the Minecraft world, like players, mobs, minecarts, and arrows. (However, most of these entity-restricted commands do not work on vehicles or projectiles.) The reason that there are somewhat different commands for the many types of Minecraft objects is because the objects in the various categories are programmed a bit differently. They have different abilities, and entities are much more complicated than most static blocks. A wolf, for example, can be "angry" (hostile), but it can also be tamed and have a collar, and you can breed it for more wolf cubs. A dirt block is pretty much just a dirt block.

Entity commands include:

/effect
/entitydata
/execute
/kill

```
/particle
/spreadplayers
/summon
/tp
```

The /effect Command

The /effect command lets you put status effects on entities (and remove effects from them), including players. For example, you can put the Blindness effect on any player entering a dark dungeon in a map you have made. Even if the player has torches, these won't help much. Look at Appendix E for a list of status effects.

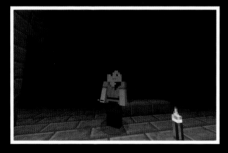

Someone with the Blindness effect can still see, but only a few blocks around them. Even if it's daylight or there are torches, everything else is black.

Syntax

```
/effect <player> <effect> [seconds]
[amplifier] [hideParticles]
```

- Replace <player> with a player's username or a target selector.

- Replace <effect> with the ID name for the status effect you want.

- May replace [seconds] with the time in seconds of how long the effect should last.

- May replace [amplifier] with the "strength" of the effect, from 0 (the lowest strength) to 255.

- May replace [hideParticles] with true or false (the default is "false"). Selecting "true" will hide the swirly particle effects from the status effect.

To remove effects use:

```
/effect <player> clear
```

Examples

```
/effect @p fire_resistance 120 2 [hideparticles]
/effect @a clear
```

The /entitydata Command

With this command, you can change data tags for an entity. For example, you can add items to a chest, change what type of armor an entity is wearing, and more.

Syntax

```
/entitydata <entity> <dataTag>
```

- Replace <entity> with a target selector for an entity.

- Replace <dataTag> with one or more dataTags and their new values.

Example

Change slimes into huge high-jumpers with the /entitydata command.

```
/entitydata @e[type=Slime]
{Motion:[0.0,1.0,0.0],Size:20}
```

The /execute Command

The /execute command is used to run commands as if another entity had run them. It can also be used to execute a command for many entities at once. /execute is a very advanced command and has many parts.

Syntax

```
/execute <entity><x><y><z><command>
```

You can also run it in detect mode, which will check for a block near the entity and only run if that block is present:

```
/execute <entity><x><y><z> detect
<x2><y2><z2><block><data><command>
```

In addition to the entity name and the XYZ coordinates, this command uses several data tags:

- Replace <entity> with an entity name or target selector.

- Replace X, Y, and Z with relative or absolute coordinates.

- Replace <command> with the command you want to run.

- In detect mode, replace X2, Y2, and Z2 with with relative or absolute coordinates.

- In detect mode, replace <block> and <data> with a block ID and data tag, or just -1 to match all.

Examples

Summon a slime on top of all existing slimes:

```
/execute @e[type=Slime] ~ ~1 ~
/summon Slime ~ ~ ~
```

Create a pool of water under all thrown snowballs:

```
/execute @e[type=Snowball] ~ ~-4 ~ /fill ~-2
~ ~-2 ~2 ~ ~2 minecraft:water 0 replace air
```

The /kill Command

This is a simple command to kill (remove) any entity, including minecarts, boats, and mobs.

Syntax

```
/kill [player|entity]
```

- With command blocks, you must replace [player| entity] with a player's name or a target selector. With the Chat window, this is optional, and typing in just /kill will kill yourself. (This can actually be handy in Creative mode—you return to your spawn quickly. Because you are in Creative, it's easy to replace your inventory items.)

Examples

```
/kill meganfair
/kill @e[type=Zombie]
/kill @e[type=!Player]
```

The /particle Command

The /particle Command allows you to create particle effects at a specified location in the world. You used to be able to target players and entities with this command, but this feature is not present in Minecraft 1.9. There is a workaround with the /execute command, covered later in this chapter.

Using a value higher than 1 for the speed of a mobSpell effect will create multicolored swirls.

Syntax

```
/particle <name> <x y z> <xd yd zd>
<speed> [count] [mode]
```

• Replace <name> with the particle ID name.

- Replace <x y z> with the coordinates of the location you want the particle effect.

- Replace <xd yd zd> with size of the area to spawn the particles: how wide (along the X axis), how tall (along the Y axis), and how wide again (along the Z axis). Using 1 1 1 here will spawn the particles in a one-block cube. (However, many of these effects use a wider area, regardless.) Also, for the reddust, mobSpell, and mobSpell Ambient, the values here will actually change the color if the [count] argument is 0 or not included.

- Replace <speed> with a number of 0 (the lowest speed) or higher to increase the speed. Generally, the faster the speed, the shorter the time you can see the effect, so slower speeds, like 0 or 0.05 are good.

- May replace [count] with a number from 0 (1 particle) up, for the total number of particles in the effect. Watch out for really high numbers here, because that can lag or even crash Minecraft. On my PC, numbers around a million started a lag for the happy villager effect, but your mileage may vary.

- May replace [mode] with either "normal" or "force" to make the particles visible by players who have set particles to be minimal in their video options. The default is "normal."

Examples

```
/particle happyVillager ~2 ~ ~2 1 1 1 .05 1000
/particle mobSpell ~2 ~1 ~ 2 3 1 1 5000
```

The /spreadplayers Command

This command will teleport a number of players into an area, all a certain distance from each other. Useful for spawning players in a mini-game!

Syntax

```
/spreadplayers <x> <z> <spreadDistance>
<maxRange> <respectTeams> <player...>
```

- Replace <x> and <z> with the coordinates of the center of the area you want players to teleport into.

- Replace <spreadDistance> with the minimum distance players can be from each other. Must be a positive number.

- Replace <maxRange> with the radius of the teleport area.

- Replace <respectTeams> with true or false. If you set it to true, it will group players by team. If not, it will be a free-for-all!

- Replace <player...> with one or more player names or a target selector. You can also target entities with this command.

Examples

```
/spreadplayers 0 0 1 10 false @a
```

The /summon Command

You can summon mobs
riding on top of other mobs,
like this stack of slimes on
top of smaller slimes.

The /summon command is a great command to play with. You can create any Minecraft entity, and even some hidden mobs you don't see in the game, like skeleton horses. When you are changing things like data tags, to give a mob enchanted armor, for example, managing the brackets correctly can be hard.

Syntax

`/summon <EntityName> [x] [y] [z] [dataTag]`

- Replace <EntityName> with the entity ID name.
- May replace [x y z] with the coordinates to summon the entity to.
- May replace [dataTag] with a data tag that is appropriate for the entity.

Examples

To summon three slimes of increasing sizes, each one riding on top of the next smallest:

```
summon Slime ~ ~2 ~
{Size:3,Passengers:[{id:"Slime",
Size:5,Passengers:[{id:"Slime",Size:7}]}]}
```

To summon a villager that will give you a diamond for each block of dirt you give him:

```
/summon Villager ~1 ~ ~
{Offers:{Recipes:[{buy:{id:dirt,Count:1},sell:
{id:diamond,Count:1},rewardExp:false}]}}
```

You can create all types of customized entities, such as this tamed zombie horse, using the /summon command.

To create a tame zombie horse with a saddle, ready to ride:

```
/summon EntityHorse ~0 ~1 ~0
{Type:3,Tame:1,SaddleItem:{id:saddle}}
```

To create an overpowered zombie with 200 health points that can cause 15 points of damage:

```
/summon Zombie ~0 ~1 ~0 {Attributes:
[{Name:generic.maxHealth,Base:200},
{Name:generic.attackDamage,Base:15}],
Health:200.0f}
```

- -

You can use the /summon command to create amazing fireworks displays. Here's an example:

```
/summon    FireworksRocketEntity   ~    ~5 ~
{LifeTime:20,   Fire-
worksItem:{id:401,Count:1,tag:
{Fireworks:{Explosions: [{Type:1,Flick-
er:1,Trail:1,Colors: [2516601],FadeCol-
ors:[3932152]}]}}}}
```

In addition to the entity name and the XYZ coordinates, this command uses several data tags:

- **Lifetime:** The number of seconds before the fireworks explosion
- Fireworks item {id:401,Count:1}, which also has tags
  - **Flicker** (true or false): for the twinkle effect
  - **Trail** (true or false): for the diamond trail effect
  - **Type**: for the shape of the explosion
  - **Colors**: for the color(s) the effect can be
  - **FadeColors**: for the colors to use as the image fades away

As you can see, nested data tags (one inside the other) make for a complicated series of brackets. And this is just one firework; you can have many inside the same command. Notice the color selection, too, uses a special format that is difficult to create. To make creating your own fireworks easier, you can use an online generator, where you can pick the shapes and colors and timing and just copy and paste the result into your own command block. One generator is at: www.minecraftupdates.com/fireworks. You can also just use a Minecraft color generator to pick your colors, like this one at http://wyattmarks.com/scripts/colorgenerator.

The /tp Command lets you or another player or entity instantly teleport somewhere in your world. You can teleport either to wherever another player is or to a specific set of coordinates. You can use command blocks to set up a teleportation hub that has buttons to teleport you to all your favorite locations.

Syntax

To send a player to the location of another player or entity:

```
/tp [target player] <destination player>
```

To send a player to a specific coordinate location:

```
/tp [target player] <x y z> [<y-rot>
<x-rot>]
```

In command blocks, you must replace [target player] with a player's name or a target selector. You will teleport yourself if you are omitting this and using the Chat window.

- Replace <destination player> with the destination player's name or a target selector.

- Replace <x y z> with the coordinates of the destination.

- May replace <y-rot> with the number of degrees of rotation horizontally (180 (to face north), -90 (east), 0 (south), 90 (west)) and <x-rot> with the number of degrees of vertical rotation (90 is facing down, -90 is facing up).

Examples

```
/tp 0 64 0
/tp meganfair megorniuspi
/tp meganfair ~10 ~ ~10 180 90
```

CHAPTER 9

PLAYER COMMANDS

Player commands work on target players. Players are a type of entity in the game programming, so you can use most entity commands on players as well. However, you can't use all player commands on entities, because not all entities are players! There are some great player commands: /give lets you give any item to a player, including weapons enchanted with higher levels than possible in the regular game.

Player commands include:

/enchant
/give
/playsound
/spawnpoint
/xp

With the /enchant command, you can enchant armor, weapons, and tools. You can only enchant one item at a time, and the item has to be in the player's hand (selected in his or her inventory). You have to stick to enchantments that are possible in the regular game though, so you can't enchant a sword with Sharpness X (10). To give a custom enchantment like that, use the /give command.

Syntax

`/enchant <player> <enchantment ID> [level]`

- Replace <player> with a player's name or target selector.

- Replace <enchantment ID> with the enchantment's ID name or number (See Appendix D for a list of enchantment IDs.)

- May replace [level] with the level of enchantment. The limit is 5, 4, 3, or 1 for many enchantments.

While the enchantments in the game use Roman numerals (like Sharpness III), here you use a regular numeral (like 1 or 3) for the level.

Examples

```
/enchant meganfair silk_touch
/enchant @p 61 3
```

The /give Command

The /give command lets you give any Minecraft item or block to a player. Because you can use data tags to modify the item you are giving, you can use this command to give items that are enchanted to a higher level than possible in the game.

Syntax

```
/give <player> <item> [amount] [data]
[dataTag]
```

- Replace <player> with a player's name or a target selector.

- Replace <item> with the block ID name or item ID name you are giving.

- May replace [amount] with the number of the item you want to give.

- May replace [data] with a data value to specify the item (for example, if you are using spruce planks instead of oak, you will need to use the data value 1).

- May replace [dataTag] with a valid data tag for the item.

With the /give command, you can give items that are enchanted with levels much higher than allowed in the game.

Examples

```
/give @a cookie 10 0
/give MegorniusPI golden_apple 1 0
{display:{Name:Apple O Life}}

/give @p golden_sword 1 0 {ench:[{id:16,lvl 7},
{id:20,lvl:5},{id:19,lvl:5}],display:
{Name:"Creepa Killa",Lore:[Burn Creepers
and Hurl Them!]}}
```

The /playsound Command

With the /playsound command, you can play one of the sounds in Minecraft to another player. For example, if you have a command block with a particle effect of an explosion going off at a fort, you could add a sound effect of the explosion with another command block. You can find a list of these sounds on the Minecraft Wiki at http://minecraft.gamepedia.com/Sounds.json#Sound_events. Some of these sound events have several different sounds that are played randomly. For example, a ghast has seven different moaning sounds, all associated with the sound event mob.ghast.moan.

Syntax

```
/playsound <sound> <player> [x y z] [volume]
[pitch] [minimumVolume]
```

- Replace <sound> with the name of the Minecraft sound event. (These are in the format category. sound.name; for example, mob.endermen.scream.)

- Replace <player> with a player's name or a target selector.

- May replace <x y z> with the location for the origin of the sound.

- May replace [volume] with a number from 0.0 up. The default is 1.0. Numbers under 1.0 are quieter and don't carry as far. For numbers above the 1.0 range, the sound carries farther.

- May replace [pitch] with a number that raises or lowers the pitch. 1.0 is the default, and numbers below this lower the pitch. Numbers above this raise the pitch.

- May replace [minimumVolume] with a number between 0 and 1 to represent how loud the sound is for players that aren't within the normal range for the sound.

Examples

```
/playsound mob.endermen.scream @p
/playsound mob.ghast.moan meganfair ~ ~ ~
1 0.1
```

Minecraft has a long list of sounds you can play with the /playsound command, including the sound of a player burping while they eat.

The /spawnpoint Command

With /spawnpoint you can set your or another player's spawn point in the world.

Syntax

`/spawnpoint [player] [x y z]`

- Must replace [player] with a player's name or a target selector if you are using command blocks. If not, you can omit this and the command will change your own spawn point.

- May replace [x y z] with the coordinates for the new spawn point. If you don't include this, the spawn point will be wherever the command is issued.

Examples

```
/spawnpoint @p ~ ~ ~
/spawnpoint MegorniusPI 500 64 -345
```

The /xp Command

The /xp command lets you give XP points or XP levels to any player.

Syntax

For points:

```
/xp <amount> [player]
```

For levels:

```
/xp <amount>L [player]
```

- Replace <amount> with the number of points or levels of XP you are giving.

- Use "L" after the <amount> (with no space before) to make this XP levels rather than points.

- Must replace [player] with a player name or target selector if you are using command blocks. Otherwise this is optional, and if you omit it, then you will get the XP points or levels.

Examples

```
/xp 30L @p
/xp 300 meganfair
```

APPENDIX A

BLOCK IDs

Blocks are objects that are placed in the Minecraft world, like cobblestone and wool blocks, as opposed to items that you use, like swords and gold ingots.

This Block ID list is a shortened list taken from the Minecraft Wiki reference and is up to date as of version 1.9. The full block ID list at the Wiki is at minecraft.gamepedia.com/Data_values/Block_IDs. Data values lists are at minecraft.gamepedia.com/Data_values. If there is a block whose ID you need that isn't on this list, visit the Minecraft Wiki. The Wiki is a fantastic public resource for all things Minecraft and is translated into many languages.

Some blocks in the same category share a block name and a block ID number. For example, blocks for stone, granite, diorite, and andesite all have the same name "stone" and the same ID "1". When you want to refer to any of these except for the default stone, you will need to include its data value (DV) number.

Also, you will find that some blocks seem categorized oddly. Because Minecraft is a continually changing game, the tactics used by developers for naming and categorizing blocks has also changed a little over time. So while Acacia Wood Stairs has its own ID name and number, Acacia Wood and Acacia Wood Planks share an ID name and number with other types of wood.

Building Blocks

	Block	ID Name	ID #	DV
	Acacia Wood Stairs	acacia_stairs	163	
	Acacia/Dark Oak Wood	log2 Variant data values: Dark Oak Wood: 1	162	*
	Bedrock	bedrock	7	
	Birch Wood Stairs	birch_stairs	135	
	Brick	brick_block	45	
	Brick Stairs	brick_stairs	108	
	Clay	clay	82	

	Name	ID	Data Value	
	Coal Block	coal_block	173	
	Coal Ore	coal_ore	16	
	Cobblestone	cobblestone	4	
	Cobblestone Stairs	stone_stairs	67	
	Dark Oak Wood Stairs	dark_oak_stairs	164	
	Diamond Block	diamond_block	57	
	Diamond Ore	diamond_ore	56	
	Dirt	dirt Variant data values: Coarse Dirt: 1; Podzol: 2	3	*
	Emerald Ore	emerald_ore	129	
	Emerald Block	emerald_block	133	
	End Stone	end_stone	121	
	Glass	glass	20	
	Glowstone	glowstone	89	
	Gold Block	gold_block	41	
	Gold Ore	gold_ore	14	
	Grass Block	grass	2	
	Gravel	gravel	13	
	Hardened Clay	hardened_clay	172	

	Ice	ice	79	
	Iron Block	iron_block	42	
	Iron Ore	iron_ore	15	
	Jungle Wood Stairs	jungle_stairs	136	
	Lapis Lazuli Block	lapis_block	22	
	Lapis Lazuli Ore	lapis_ore	21	
	Moss Stone	mossy_cobblestone	48	
	Mycelium	mycelium	110	
	Nether Brick	nether_brick	112	
	Nether Quartz Ore	quartz_ore	153	
	Netherrack	netherrack	87	
	Oak Wood Stairs	oak_stairs	53	
	Obsidian	obsidian	49	
	Packed Ice	packed_ice	174	
	Prismarine	prismarine Variant data values: Prismarine bricks (1); Dark Prismarine (2)	168	*
	Quartz Block	quartz_block Variant data values: Chiseled Quartz (1); Pillar Quartz (2)	155	*
	Quartz Stairs	quartz_stairs	156	

	Red Sandstone	red_sandstone Variant data values: Chiseled Red Sandstone: 1; Smooth Red Sandstone: 2	179	
	Red Sandstone Slab	stone_slab2	182	
	Red Sandstone Stairs	red_sandstone_stairs	180	
	Redstone Block	redstone_block	152	
	Redstone Ore	redstone_ore	73	
	Sand	sand Variant data values: Red sand: 1	12	0
	Sandstone	sandstone Variant data values: Chiseled Sandstone: 1; Smooth Sandstone: 2.	24	
	Sandstone Stairs	sandstone_stairs	128	
	Sea Lantern	sea_lantern	169	
	Snow (block)	snow	80	
	Soul Sand	soul_sand	88	
	Spruce Wood Stairs	spruce_stairs	134	
	Stained Clay	stained_hardened_clay Variant data values: Orange: 1; Magenta: 2; Light Blue: 3; Yellow: 4; Lime: 5; Pink: 6; Gray: 7; Light Gray: 8; Cyan: 9; Purple: 10; Blue: 11; Brown: 12; Green: 13; Red: 14; and Black: 15	159	*

	Stained Glass (white)	stained_glass Variant data values: Orange: 1; Magenta: 2; Light Blue: 3; Yellow: 4; Lime: 5; Pink: 6; Gray: 7; Light Gray: 8; Cyan: 9; Purple: 10; Blue: 11; Brown: 12; Green: 13; Red: 14; and Black: 15	95	*
	Stained Glass Pane	stained_glass_pane Variant data values: Orange: 1; Magenta: 2; Light Blue: 3; Yellow: 4; Lime: 5; Pink: 6; Gray: 7; Light Gray: 8; Cyan: 9; Purple: 10; Blue: 11; Brown: 12; Green: 13; Red: 14; and Black: 15	160	*
	Stone	stone Variant data values: Granite: 1; Polished Granite: 2; Diorite: 3; Polished Diorite: 4: Andesite: 5; Polished Andesite: 6	1	*
	Stone Brick	stonebrick Variant data values: Mossy Stone Brick: 1; Cracked Stone Brick: 2; Chiseled Stone Brick: 3	98	*
	Stone Brick Stairs	stone_brick_stairs	109	
	Stone Slab	stone_slab Variant data values: Sandstone Slab:1; Wooden Slab: 2; Cobblestone Slab:3; Brick Slab: 4; Stone Brick Slab: 5; Nether Brick Slab: 6; Quartz Slab: 7	44	*

	Block	ID Name	ID #	DV
	Wood (Oak)	log Variant data values: Spruce: 1; Birch: 2; Jungle: 3; Acacia: 4; Dark Oak: 5	17	*
	Wood Planks (Oak)	planks Variant data values: Spruce: 1; Birch: 2; Jungle: 3; Acacia: 4; Dark Oak: 5	5	*
	Wooden Slab (Oak)	wooden_slab Variant data values: Spruce: 1; Birch: 2; Jungle: 3; Acacia: 4; Dark Oak: 5	126	*
	Wool	wool Variant data values: Orange: 1; Magenta: 2; Light Blue: 3; Yellow: 4; Lime: 5; Pink: 6; Gray: 7; Light Gray: 8; Cyan: 9; Purple: 10; Blue: 11; Brown: 12; Green: 13; Red: 14; and Black: 15	35	*

Decoration Blocks

	Block	ID Name	ID #	DV
	Bookshelf	bookshelf	47	
	Carpet (white)	carpet Variant data values: Orange: 1; Magenta: 2; Light Blue: 3; Yellow: 4; Lime: 5; Pink: 6; Gray: 7;	171	

		Light Gray: 8; Cyan: 9; Purple: 10; Blue: 11; Brown: 12; Green: 13; Red: 14; and Black: 15		
	Cobweb	web	30	
	Flower Pot	flower_pot	140	
	Glass Pane	glass_pane	102	
	Hay Bale	hay_block	170	
	Iron Bars	iron_bars	101	
	Mob head (skeleton)	skull Variant data values: Wither skeleton: 1; Zombie: 2; Steve: 3; Creeper: 4.	144	
	Snow (layer)	snow_layer	78	

Fences, Gates, and Doors

	Block	ID Name	ID#	DV
	Acacia Door	acacia_door	196	
	Acacia Fence	acacia_fence	192	
	Acacia Fence Gate	acacia_fence_gate	187	
	Birch Door	birch_door	194	

	Name	ID	Number	
	Birch Fence	birch_fence	189	
	Birch Fence Gate	birch_fence_gate	184	
	Cobblestone Wall	cobblestone_wall For a mossy cobble wall, use data value 1	139	
	Dark Oak Door	dark_oak_door	197	
	Dark Oak Fence	dark_oak_fence	191	
	Dark Oak Fence Gate	dark_oak_fence_gate	186	
	Fence (oak)	fence	85	
	Fence Gate (oak)	fence_gate	107	
	Jungle Door	jungle_door	195	
	Jungle Fence	jungle_fence	190	
	Jungle Fence Gate	jungle_fence_gate	185	
	Nether Brick Fence	nether_brick_fence	113	
	Nether Brick Stairs	nether_brick_stairs	114	
	Spruce Door	spruce_door	193	
	Spruce Fence	spruce_fence	188	
	Spruce Fence Gate	spruce_fence_gate	183	
	Wood Door (oak)	wooden_door	64	

Miscellaneous

	Block	ID Name	ID #	DV
–	Air	air	0	
	Anvil	anvil	145	
	Barrier	barrier	166	
	Bed	bed	26	
	Brewing Stand	brewing_stand	117	
	Cake	cake	92	
	Cauldron	cauldron	118	
	Chest	chest	54	
	Command Block	command_block	137	
	Crafting Table	crafting_table	58	
	Enchantment Table	enchanting_table	116	
	Furnace	furnace	61	
	Jukebox	jukebox	84	
	Note Block	noteblock	25	
	Piston	piston	33	
	Slime Block	slime	165	
	Sponge	sponge Variant data value: Wet Sponge: 1	19	

	Block	ID Name	ID #	DV
	TNT	tnt	46	
	Torch	torch	50	

	Block	ID Name	ID #	DV
	Acacia/Dark Oak Leaves	leaves2 Variant data values: Dark Oak: 1	161	*
	Allium	red_flower	38	2
	Azure Bluet	red_flower	38	3
	Blue Orchid	red_flower	38	1
	Brown Mushroom	brown_mushroom	39	
	Brown Mushroom (block)	brown_mushroom_block	99	
	Cactus	cactus	81	
	Cocoa	cocoa	127	
	Dandelion	yellow_flower	37	
	Dead Bush	deadbush	32	
	Double Tall-grass	double_plant	175	2
	Fern	tallgrass	31	2

	Grass	tallgrass	31	1
	Jack o'Lantern	lit_pumpkin	91	
	Large Fern	double_plant	175	3
	Leaves (oak)	leaves Variant data values: 1-3: Spruce: 1; Birch: 2; Jungle: 3	18	*
	Lilac	double_plant	175	1
	Lily Pad	waterlily	111	
	Melon	melon_block	103	
	Nether Wart (block)	nether_wart	115	
	Orange Tulip	red_flower	38	5
	Oxeye Daisy	red_flower	38	8
	Peony	double_plant	175	5
	Pink Tulip	red_flower	38	7
	Poppy	red_flower	38	0
	Pumpkin	pumpkin	86	
	Red Mushroom	red_mushroom	40	
	Red Mushroom (block)	red_mushroom_block	100	
	Red Tulip	red_flower	38	4
	Rose Bush	double_plant	175	4

	Sapling (Oak)	sapling Variant data values: Spruce: 1; Birch : 2; Jungle: 3; Acacia: 4; Dark Oak: 5	6	*
	Sugar Cane (block)	reeds	83	
	Sunflower	double_plant	175	
	Vines	vine	106	
	White Tulip	red_flower	38	6

APPENDIX 8

ITEM IDs

Minecraft items are things that you use or wear, like tools and weapons, rather than place in the world (although some items are placeable, like brewing stands). While block ID numbers are all below 255, item ID numbers are all above 255. As with block IDs, some similar items, like different dyes, share the same ID number but have different data value IDs.

This is a shortened list taken from the Minecraft Wiki refer ence. The full item ID list at the Wiki is at minecraft.gamepedia. com/Data_values/Item_IDs. Data values lists are at minecraft. gamepedia.com/Data_values. If there is an item whose ID you need that isn't on this list, visit the Minecraft Wiki. In addition, some Minecraft objects have both block and item IDs.

	Item	ID Name	ID Number
	Armor Stand	armor_stand	416
	Chain Boots	chainmail_boots	305
	Chain Chestplate	chainmail_chestplate	303
	Chain Helmet	chainmail_helmet	302
	Chain Leggings	chainmail_leggings	304
	Diamond Boots	diamond_boots	313
	Diamond Chestplate	diamond_chestplate	311
	Diamond Helmet	diamond_helmet	310
	Diamond Leggings	diamond_leggings	312
	Golden Boots	golden_boots	317
	Golden Chestplate	golden_chestplate	315
	Golden Helmet	golden_helmet	314
	Golden Leggings	golden_leggings	316
	Horse Armor (Diamond)	diamond_horse_armor	419
	Horse Armor (Golden)	golden_horse_armor	418
	Horse Armor (Iron)	iron_horse_armor	417
	Iron Boots	iron_boots	309

	Item	ID Name	ID Number
	Iron Chestplate	iron_chestplate	307
	Iron Helmet	iron_helmet	306
	Iron Leggings	iron_leggings	308
	Leather Boots	leather_boots	301
	Leather Cap	leather_helmet	298
	Leather Pants	leather_leggings	300
	Leather Tunic	leather_chestplate	299

Food and Plant-related

	Item	ID Name	ID Number
	Apple	apple	260
	Baked Potato	baked_potato	393
	Beef (Raw)	beef	363
	Bread	bread	297
	Cake	cake	354
	Carrot	carrot	391
	Chicken (Raw)	chicken	365
	Chicken (Cooked)	cooked_chicken	366

	Cookie	cookie	357
	Fish (Raw)	fish	349
	Fish (Cooked)	cooked_fish	350
	Golden Apple	golden_apple	322
	Golden Carrot	golden_carrot	396
	Melon	melon	360
	Melon Seeds	melon_seeds	362
	Milk	milk_bucket	335
	Mushroom Stew	mushroom_stew	282
	Mutton (Cooked)	cooked_mutton	424
	Mutton (Raw)	mutton	423
	Porkchop (Cooked)	cooked_porkchop	320
	Porkchop (Raw)	porkchop	319
	Potato	potato	392
	Poisonous Potato	poisonous_potato	394
	Pumpkin Pie	pumpkin_pie	400
	Pumpkin Seeds	pumpkin_seeds	361
	Rabbit (Cooked)	cooked_rabbit	412
	Rabbit (Raw)	rabbit	411
	Rabbit Stew	rabbit_stew	413

	Item	ID Name	ID Number
	Rotten Flesh	rotten_flesh	367
	Seeds	wheat_seeds	295
	Steak	cooked_beef	364
	Sugar	sugar	353
	Wheat	wheat	296

Household and Miscellaneous Goods

	Item	ID Name	ID Number
	Banner	banner	425
	Bed	bed	355
	Birch Door	birch_door	428
	Boat	boat	333
	Book	book	340
	Book and Quill	writable_book	386
	Bottle o' Enchanting	experience_bottle	384
	Bowl	bowl	281
	Bucket	bucket	325
	Carrot on a Stick	carrot_on_a_stick	398

	Empty Map	map	395
	Enchanted Book	enchanted_book	403
	Fire Charge	fire_charge	385
−	Firework Rocket	fireworks	401
	Firework Star	firework_charge	402
	Glass Bottle	glass_bottle	374
	Iron Door	iron_door	330
	Item Frame	item_frame	389
	Jungle Door	jungle_door	429
	Minecart	minecart	328
	Oak Door	wooden_door	324
	Painting	painting	321
	Paper	paper	339
	Potion (Water Bottle) *For specific potions, see Appendix H: Potion IDs	potion	373
	Saddle	saddle	329
	Sign	sign	323
	Spawn Egg	spawn_egg	383
	Spruce Door	spruce_door	427
	Stick	stick	280

Materials and Mob Drops

	Item	ID Name	ID Number
	Blaze Powder	blaze_powder	377
	Blaze Rod	blaze_rod	369
	Bone	bone	352
	Brick	brick	336
	Clay	clay_ball	337
	Coal	coal	263
	Diamond	diamond	264
	Dye (Ink Sac) *bonemeal	dye	351
	Egg	egg	344
	Emerald	emerald	388
	Ender Pearl	ender_pearl	368
	Eye of Ender	ender_eye	381
	Feather	feather	288
	Fermented Spider Eye	fermented_spider_eye	376
	Flint	flint	318
	Ghast Tear	ghast_tear	370
	Glistering Melon	speckled_melon	382

	Glowstone Dust	glowstone_dust	348
	Gold Ingot	gold_ingot	266
	Gold Nugget	gold_nugget	371
	Gunpowder	gunpowder	289
	Iron Ingot	iron_ingot	265
	Lava Bucket	lava_bucket	327
	Leather	leather	334
	Magma Cream	magma_cream	378
	Mob Head	skull	397
	Nether Brick	netherbrick	405
	Nether Quartz	quartz	406
	Nether Star	nether_star	399
	Nether Wart	nether_wart	372
	Prismarine Shard	prismarine_shard	409
	Prismarine Crystals	prismarine_crystals	410
	Rabbit's Foot	rabbit_foot	414
	Rabbit Hide	rabbit_hide	415
	Redstone	redstone	331
	Slimeball	slime_ball	341
	Snowball	snowball	332

	Spider Eye	spider_eye	375
	String	string	287
	Sugar Cane	reeds	338
	Water Bucket	water_bucket	326

Music Disc ID Names and Numbers

	Item	ID Name	ID Number
	11 Disc	record_11	2266
	13 Disc	record_13	2256
	Blocks Disc	record_blocks	2258
	Cat Disc	record_cat	2257
	Chirp Disc	record_chirp	2259
	Far Disc	record_far	2260
	Mall Disc	record_mall	2261
	Mellohi Disc	record_mellohi	2262
	Stal Disc	record_stal	2263
	Strad Disc	record_strad	2264
	Wait Disc	record_wait	2267
	Ward Disc	record_ward	2265

	Item	ID Name	ID Number
	Clock	clock	347
	Compass	compass	345
	Diamond Axe	diamond_axe	279
	Diamond Hoe	diamond_hoe	293
	Diamond Pickaxe	diamond_pickaxe	278
	Diamond Shovel	diamond_shovel	277
	Fishing Rod	fishing_rod	346
	Flint and Steel	flint_and_steel	259
	Golden Axe	golden_axe	286
	Golden Hoe	golden_hoe	294
	Golden Pickaxe	golden_pickaxe	285
	Golden Shovel	golden_shovel	284
	Iron Axe	iron_axe	258
	Iron Hoe	iron_hoe	292
	Iron Pickaxe	iron_pickaxe	257
	Iron Shovel	iron_shovel	256
	Lead	lead	420
	Name Tag	name_tag	421

	Item	ID Name	ID Number
	Shears	shears	359
	Stone Axe	stone_axe	275
	Stone Hoe	stone_hoe	291
	Stone Pickaxe	stone_pickaxe	274
	Stone Shovel	stone_shovel	273
	Wooden Axe	wooden_axe	271
	Wooden Hoe	wooden_hoe	290
	Wooden Pickaxe	wooden_pickaxe	270
	Wooden Shovel	wooden_shovel	269

Weapons

	Item	ID Name	ID Number
	Arrow	arrow	262
	Bow	bow	261
	Diamond Sword	diamond_sword	276
	Golden Sword	golden_sword	283
	Iron Sword	iron_sword	267
	Wooden Sword	wooden_sword	268

POTION IDs

All of these potions have the ID name "potion" and the ID number "373" so you use their data value to specify which potion you want. After the potion name is the length of time that the potion is in effect; otherwise the potion is instant.

Potion	Data Value
Awkward Potion	16
Fire Resistance Potion (3:00)	8195
Fire Resistance Potion (8:00)	8259
Fire Resistance Splash (2:15)	16387
Fire Resistance Splash (6:00)	16451
Harming Potion	8204

Harming Potion II	8236
Harming Splash	16396
Harming Splash II	16428
Healing Potion	8197
Healing Potion II	8229
Healing Splash	16389
Healing Splash II	16421
Invisibility Potion (3:00)	8206
Invisibility Potion (8:00)	8270
Invisibility Splash (2:15)	16398
Invisibility Splash (6:00)	16462
Leaping Potion (3:00)	8267
Leaping Potion II (1:30)	8235
Leaping Splash (2:15)	16459
Leaping Splash II (1:07)	16427
Night Vision Potion (3:00)	8198
Night Vision Potion (8:00)	8262
Night Vision Splash (2:15)	16390
Night Vision Splash (6:00)	16454
Poison Potion (0:45)	8196
Poison Potion (2:00)	8260
Poison Potion II (0:22)	8228
Poison Potion II (1:00)	8292
Poison Splash (0:33)	16388
Poison Splash (1:30)	16452
Poison Splash II (0:16)	16420
Poison Splash II (0:45)	16484
Regeneration Potion (0:45)	8193
Regeneration Potion (2:00)	8257
Regeneration Potion II (0:22)	8225
Regeneration Potion II (1:00)	8289

Regeneration Splash (0:33)	16385
Regeneration Splash (1:30)	16449
Regeneration Splash II (0:16)	16417
Regeneration Splash II (0:45)	16481
Slowness Potion (1:30)	8202
Slowness Potion (4:00)	8266
Slowness Splash (1:07)	16394
Slowness Splash (3:00)	16458
Strength Potion (3:00)	8201
Strength Potion (8:00)	8265
Strength Potion II (1:30)	8233
Strength Potion II (4:00)	8297
Strength Splash (2:15)	16393
Strength Splash (6:00)	16457
Strength Splash II (1:07)	16425
Strength Splash II (3:00)	16489
Swiftness Potion (3:00)	8194
Swiftness Potion (8:00)	8258
Swiftness Potion II (1:30)	8226
Swiftness Potion II (4:00)	8290
Swiftness Splash (2:15)	16386
Swiftness Splash (6:00)	16450
Swiftness Splash II (1:07)	16418
Swiftness Splash II (3:00)	16482
Water Breathing Potion (3:00)	8205
Water Breathing Potion (8:00)	8269
Water Breathing Splash (2:15)	16397
Water Breathing Splash (6:00)	16461
Weakness Potion (1:30)	8200
Weakness Potion (4:00)	8264
Weakness Splash (1:07)	16392
Weakness Splash (3:00)	16456

ENCHANTMENT IDs

hese IDs are used with the /give command and the /enchant command. The Highest Level is the maximum level the enchantment can have in regular gameplay.

Enchantment	Name	ID	Highest Level
Protection	protection	0	IV
Fire Protection	fire_protection	1	IV
Feather Falling	feather_falling	2	IV
Blast Protection	blast_protection	3	IV
Projectile Protection	projectile_protection	4	IV
Respiration	respiration	5	III

Aqua Affinity	aqua_affinity	6	I
Thorns	thorns	7	III
Depth Strider	depth_strider	8	III
Sharpness	sharpness	16	V
Smite	smite	17	V
Bane of Arthropods	bane_of_arthropods	18	V
Knockback	knockback	19	II
Fire Aspect	fire_aspect	20	II
Looting	looting	21	III
Efficiency	efficiency	32	V
Silk Touch	silk_touch	33	I
Unbreaking	unbreaking	34	III
Fortune	fortune	35	III
Power	power	48	V
Punch	punch	49	II
Flame	flame	50	I
Infinity	infinity	51	I
Luck of the Sea	luck_of_the_sea	61	III
Lure	lure	62	III

STATUS EFFECTS

	Status Effect	**ID Name**	**ID #**
🖐	Speed	speed	1
⚫	Slowness	slowness	2
⛏	Haste	haste	3
🗝	Mining Fatigue	mining_fatigue	4

	Strength	strength	5
–	Instant Health	instant_health	6
–	Instant Damage	instant_damage	7
	Jump Boost	jump_boost	8
	Nausea	nausea	9
	Regeneration	regeneration	10
	Resistance	resistance	11
	Fire Resistance	fire_resistance	12
	Water Breathing	water_breathing	13
	Invisibility	invisibility	14
	Blindness	blindness	15
	Night vision	night_vision	16
	Hunger	hunger	17
	Weakness	weakness	18
	Poison	poison	19
	Wither	wither	20
	Health Boost	health_boost	21
	Absorption	absorption	22
–	Saturation	saturation	23

APPENDIX F

PARTICLES

U se these ID names for visual effects with the /particle command.

This is a shortened version of the full particle list at the Minecraft Wiki. For the full list, visit minecraft.gamepedia.com/Particles

angryVillager	dripWater
bubble (only works	dripLava
underwater)	droplet
cloud	enchantmenttable
crit	explode

fireworksSpark	portal
flame	reddust
happyVillager	slime
heart	smoke
hugeexplosion	snowballpoof
instantSpell	snowshovel
largeexplode	spell
largesmoke	splash
lava	wake
magicCrit	witchMagic
mobSpell	
note	

APPENDIX C

ENTITY IDS

You refer to entities by their ID name, which is also called their Savegame ID. This is a slightly shortened list of the full entity ID list at the Minecraft Wiki, which you can find here: minecraft.gamepedia.com/Data_values/Entity_IDs

Entity	ID Name (Savegame ID)
Bat	Bat
Blaze	Blaze
Cave Spider	CaveSpider
Chicken	Chicken
Cow	Cow
Creeper	Creeper
Ender Dragon	EnderDragon

Entity	ID Name (Savegame ID)
Enderman	Enderman
Endermite	Endermite
Experience Orb	XPOrb
Falling Block (gravel, sand, anvil, dragon egg)	FallingSand
Firework Rocket	FireworksRocketEntity
Giant	Giant
Ghast	Ghast
Guardian	Guardian
Horse	EntityHorse
Iron Golem	VillagerGolem
Killer Rabbit	Rabbit
Magma Cube	LavaSlime
Mooshroom	MushroomCow
Ocelot	Ozelot
Pig	Pig
Primed TNT	PrimedTnt
Rabbit	Rabbit
Sheep	Sheep
Silverfish	Silverfish
Skeleton	Skeleton
Slime	Slime
Snow Golem	SnowMan
Spider	Spider
Squid	Squid
Villager	Villager
Witch	Witch
Wither	WitherBoss
Wolf	Wolf
Zombie Villager	Zombie
Zombie Pigman	PigZombie

APPENDIX H

COMMANDS

This list covers most Minecraft commands, but not server administration commands. To learn more about commands that manage a server, visit the Minecraft Wiki at minecraft. gamepedia.com/Commands.

Italics show the text that must be replaced. The angle brackets show parameters that must be included, and the square brackets show optional parameters. (These brackets shouldn't be included in the command.) Also, the commands and syntax below start with a slash. The slash is required for commands used in the Chat window but optional for commands used in a command block.

Command	Syntax
/achievement	`/achievement <give|take> <stat_name|*> [player]`
/blockdata	`/blockdata <x y z> <dataTag>`
/clear	`/clear [player] [item] [data] [maxCount] [dataTag]`
/clone	`/clone <x1 y1 z1> <x2 y2 z2> <x y z> [maskMode] [cloneMode] [TileName]`
/defaultgamemode	`/defaultgamemode <mode>`
/difficulty	`/difficulty <new difficulty>`

/effect	`/effect <player> <effect> [seconds] [amplifier] [hideParticles]`
	
	`/effect <player> clear`

/enchant	`/enchant <player> <enchantment ID> [level]`
/entitydata	`/entitydata <entity> <dataTag>`

/execute	`/execute <entity> <x y z> <command>`
	
	`/execute <entity> <x y z> detect <x2 y2 z2> <block> <data> <command>`

/fill	`/fill <x1 y1 z1> <x2 y2 <z2> <TileName> [dataValue] [oldBlockHandling] [dataTag]`
	
	`/fill <x1 y1 z1> <x2 y2 z2> <TileName> <dataValue> replace [replaceTileName] [replaceDataValue]`

/gamemode	`/gamemode <mode> [player]`

Command	Syntax
/gamerule	/gamerule <rule name> [value]
/give	/give <player> <item> [amount] [data] [dataTag]
/help	/help [page|command name] /? [page|command name]
/kill	/kill [player|entity]
/list	/list
/me	/me <action …>
/particle	/particle <name> <x y z> <xd yd zd> <speed> [count] [mode]
/playsound	/playsound <sound> <player> [x y z] [volume] [pitch] [minimumVolume]
/replaceitem	/replaceitem block <x y z> <slot> <item> [amount] [data] [dataTag] /replaceitem entity <selector> <slot> <item> [amount] [data] [dataTag]
/say	/say <message …>
/scoreboard	/scoreboard <objectives|players|teams> …
/seed	/seed
/setblock	/setblock <x y z> <TileName> [dataValue] [oldBlockHandling] [dataTag]
/setworldspawn	/setworldspawn [x y z]
/spawnpoint	/spawnpoint [player] [x y z]
/spreadplayers	/spreadplayers <x z> <spreadDistance> <maxRange> <respectTeams> <player …>

Command	Syntax
/stats	`/stats block <x y z> clear <stat>`
	`/stats block <x y z> set <stat> <selector><objective>`
	`/stats entity <selector2> clear <stat>`
	`/stats entity <selector2> set <stat> <selector> <objective>`
/summon	`/summon <EntityName> [x y z] [dataTag]`
/tell	`/tell <player> <private message ...>`
	`/msg <player> <private message ...>`
	`/w <player> <private message ...>`
/tellraw	`/tellraw <player> <raw json message>`
/testfor	`/testfor <player> [dataTag]`
/testforblock	`/testforblock <x y z> <TileName> [dataValue] [dataTag]`
/testforblocks	`/testforblocks <x1 y1 z1> <x2 y2 z2> <x y z> [mode]`
/time	`/time <add|query|set> <value>`
/title	`/title <player> clear`
	`/title <player> reset`
	`/title <player> subtitle <raw json title>`
	`/title <player> times <fadeIn> <stay> <fadeOut>`
	`/title <player> title <raw json title>`

Command	Syntax
/toggledownfall	/toggledownfall
/tp	/tp [target player] <destination player> /tp [target player] <x y z> [<y-rot x-rot>]
/trigger	/trigger <objective> <add|set> <value>
/weather	/weather <clear|rain|thunder> [duration in seconds]
/worldborder	/worldborder add <sizeInBlocks> [timeInSeconds] /worldborder center <x z> /worldborder damage amount <damagePerBlock> /worldborder damage buffer <sizeInBlocks> /worldborder get /worldborder set <sizeInBlocks> [timeInSeconds] /worldborder warning distance <blocks> /worldborder warning time <seconds>
/xp	/xp <amount> [player] /xp <amount>L [player]

*Source: Minecraft Wiki at minecraft.gamepedia.com/Commands and the Minecraft 1.9 game.